Farm Animals

SHEEP ON THE FARM

By Rose Carraway

Gareth Stevens
Publishing

Please visit our website, www.garethstevens.com. For a free color catalog of all our
high-quality books, call toll free 1-800-542-2595 or fax 1-877-542-2596.

Library of Congress Cataloging-in-Publication Data

Carraway, Rose.
Sheep on the farm / Rose Carraway.
p. cm. — (Farm animals)
Includes index.
ISBN 978-1-4339-7365-9 (pbk.)
ISBN 978-1-4339-7366-6 (6-pack)
ISBN 978-1-4339-7364-2 (library binding)
1. Sheep—Juvenile literature. I. Title.
SF375.2.C37 2013
636.3'1—dc23

2011051820

First Edition

Published in 2013 by
Gareth Stevens Publishing
111 East 14th Street, Suite 349
New York, NY 10003

Copyright © 2013 Gareth Stevens Publishing

Editor: Katie Kawa
Designer: Andrea Davison-Bartolotta

Photo credits: Cover, pp. 1, 15 1000 Words/Shutterstock.com; p. 5 Pete Pahham/Shutterstock.com; pp. 7, 24
(flock) Pichugin Dmitry/Shutterstock.com; p. 9 Antonina Potapenko/Shutterstock.com; p. 11 Katrina Leigh/
Shutterstock.com; p. 13 Sandra Peek/Shutterstock.com; p. 17 iStockphoto/Thinkstock; p. 19 Digital Vision/
Thinkstock; pp. 21, 24 (wool) Birgit Urban/Shutterstock.com; p. 23 kavring/Shutterstock.com.

Printed in the United States of America

CPSIA compliance information: Batch #CS12GS: For further information contact Gareth Stevens, New York, New York at 1-800-542-2595.

Contents

Sheep are shy animals.

Sheep stay in a group for safety. The group is called a flock.

A baby sheep is a lamb. Lambs are born in the spring.

Dogs help farmers
move sheep.

A sheep makes a noise called a bleat.

Sheep eat grass.

15

They eat hay
in the winter.

Farmers get milk
from sheep.

Sheep have soft hair.
It is called wool.

Wool is used
to make clothes.

Words to Know

flock

wool

Index